Everyone Just Wants to Drum

Poems by Kevin Rabas

Spartan Press
Kansas City   Missouri

Spartan Press
Kansas City, MO
spartanpresskc@gmail.com

Copyright © Kevin Rabas, 2019
First Edition 1 3 5 7 9 10 8 6 4 2
ISBN: 978-1-950380-03-9
LCCN: 2019932565

Design, edits and layout: Jason Ryberg
Cover photograph and author photo: Dave Leiker
Cover design: Eric Sonnakolb
All rights reserved. No part of this publication may be reproduced or transmitted in any form or by any means, electronic or mechanical, including photocopying, recording or by info retrieval system, without prior written permission from the author.

The author gratefully acknowledges the editors of the following publications in which versions of the following poems first appeared:

"Shot of Water" in *The Fenland Reed*.
"Jazz Standards" in *Yellow Mama Webzine*.

Thanks to my hand models, who drummed together to help get a photo shot for this book's cover. Hand models: Maximilian Miranda, Joaquin Miranda, Irene Díaz, Jason Buck, Linzi Garcia, Eliot Rabas and Lisa Moritz.

Thanks to the following for curating the poems that make up this book, Michael Pelletier and Linzi Garcia.

Thanks to Jason Ryberg—friend, poetic brother, editor, literary raconteur.

TABLE OF CONTENTS

Kids

    Always Cling / 1
    Flossing / 2
    Shot of Water / 3
    Magic Rabbits / 4
    Chess Bets / 5
    Cycle Broken / 6
    Hockey / 7
    With a Stick / 8
    Evenings at the Pool / 9
    E, Back from Mission Trip / 10
    Golden Boy / 11
    Wind in the Wheat / 12
    Scary Ride / 13
    Baptism Sketch / 14
    Easy for Me / 15
    Trees Have Bark / 16

Music

    That Kind of Quiet / 18
    Improv / 19
    Jazz Standards / 20
    Crazy / 21
    Know Those Notes / 22
    How composed music hopes / 23
    When you carry in drums / 24
    Quartet / 25
    Cadenza / 26
    House Rule / 27

Disquiet
    Mom Brings My Drum to Menninger's / 30
    Anti-D / 31
    Take One, Take Two / 32
    Chipping, Backyard Golf / 33
    Moving / 34

Time Off
    Meet me at the coffee shop, or victory lap / 36
    Snowed in in NYC, Vacation Extended / 37
    Off the Clock / 38
    Alamo, KC / 39
    On the Road / 40
    Rush Hour Break / 41
    Seven Minute Break / 42

Words, Language
    Translation / 44
    Word Bank / 45
    Not Blocked / 46
    His Sentence / 47
    Dialogue, Monologue / 48
    Underwater / 49
    On the train to the reading / 50
    Dirty Kanza / 51
    Theatre Going / 52
    I'd Like to Write / 53

Prose Sketches
    Everyone Just Wants to Drum / 56
    Relic / 57
    Write for an Hour at the Office / 58
    About that time we left the locker room
        through a cloud / 59

Song Cycle: Poems at the Piano
    Missing Moon / 62
    Staccato Beans / 63
    Herd Boy's Song / 64
    Blue Nun / 65
    Ancient Burial / 66
    Floating Clouds / 67
    Red Wilderness / 68
    Sunrain / 69

At the Gym, the Gas Station, the Coffee Shop
    Curls / 72
    Grunt / 73
    Power / 74
    Gas Station / 75
    Gas Station Window Spot / 76
    Outside the Starbucks / 77
    How to Coffee Shop / 78
    Endless Iced Tea / 79
    Our Songs / 80

Observations
    Hum / 82
    In the Well / 83
    That afternoon … / 84
    Commencement / 85
    Snow for Easter / 86
    Rain Day / 87
    Hail / 88
    Now & Now & Now / 89
    Instances / 90
    More Than / 91
    Branch, *The Learning Tree* / 92
    Reincarnate / 93

for Lisa

Kids

Always Cling

At the soda fountain,
   the little girl
holds, clamped
to her mother's side
   arm around her neck,
legs around her mother's
   middle, mother's waist,
little monkey, little one,
   we've been holding
together, like this, for hundreds,
thousands of years—
in the tangled forests, in the tall
tan grass, among the jutting mountains.
   May we always,
     always cling.

Flossing

Ethan, 9, dances
in the stands at The K
his hands and elbows pumping,
his hips jittering, like he's
flossing his bum
with an invisible towel.

Alicia: Ethan, are you gonna teach
   Grandma how to floss?
Grandma: Just not right now.
Alicia: That'd totally get you both
   on the stadium camera.

The K: Kauffman Stadium, home of the Kansas City Royals

Shot of Water

When I was little, and rode in father's pickup truck,
his faded blue El Camino, the bumper
bent in like a smile, Dad would say,
Gimme a little shot of that water,
son, and I'd hand him the red and white thermos,
the day hot, the windows rolled
all the way down, his hand
on the wheel, tanned and dark copper,
rust colored, hairy. Father worked construction.
Drove me to softball practice
after work. I did what he said.

Magic Rabbits

And with that wave of the hand, the fire went out
   and the rabbits popped from the silver-lidded pan,
magic. I'd been practicing this trick
   in front of the cats, the potted plants,
the TV, until I could do the trick, move
   through the motions, with my eyes
both opened or closed, and each morning
   I left the house, stark sun or grey ice and snow,
with a yellow water pitcher and a sack
   of food for those rabbits,
who got the bright stage lights
   just once a month, and the rest
of the time lived in a wooden hutch
   out back that my dad built.
We'd scoop their round poops
   into the garden.

Chess Bets

On the comic book cover
   Logan's on a metal table,
wires across his body,
red & blue & green. Mom says,
That one's too weird, too violent,
   and so I can't get it.
At school, we take apart the tangrams,
   use the pieces to play chess,
who wins gets a comic, we
   bet. I wager
my Spider-Man against Jason Stott's
   Wolverine.

*Logan (James Howlett) becomes Wolverine.

Cycle Broken

I can't know
what it was
in Bud's house
at the end of the street, how he
came at me one day, fists up,
chest out, eyes like hot coals,
and I flipped him in the grass
and even lent a hand up.
He called me *karate cricket*
after that, but I know
at home Bud's Dad also
put up fists, or slammed them down,
or put them into the table
or the side of Bud's face. Bud came
at me wanting something back,
something back from the world, the block,
the other kids. My father's father
used his fists. My mother said,
Not with him.

Hockey

Never been in a fight
  on the ice, but I like
how you take the puck
  or take the body, take one
or the other out of play.
    I started at 5, & we weren't
allowed to hit till I was 11.
    The game just goes and goes,
no stops, until the whistle.
    Never lost
      a tooth.

With a Stick

If I were on your block
   when I was young, I'd
have been a littler kid,
   but one unafraid
      of dogs, one
who'd come
   with a stick, help
you get by, help you
   down the block
      and into the field.

Evenings at the Pool

That summer, we decided to go to the pool
   evenings after work and sit in the sun
and watch its rays sink
   into the blue blue water.

I'd spent every evening this way
   when I was young, a lifeguard
on the stand, my feet high above
   the water.

Sometimes, we'd hold hands
   and watch our son swim.
Three years, and he'll be in college.
   Who will watch him then?

E, Back from Mission Trip

When our son comes home
from mission trip, a few weeks
painting, hammering against
that hurricane wreck,
a Kansan down south,
where the water
rolls big in waves
and never seems to end,

who will he be
once he's home?

Golden Boy

written with Ramiro Miranda

My son has this alter ego,
a second self, Golden Boy.
  My son says,
Remember that time
  Golden Boy took Chompy
for a walk, and we found
  cash in the grass?

When I cannot get through
  to my son, I say,
What do you think
  Golden Boy would do?

My son says,
  I'll ask him.

Wind in the Wheat

with Kevin Johnson

When I lived in Derby
   the last two weeks of May
before the wheat was harvested
   I'd bike out to where
wheat was on both sides
   of the road, dirt road,
the wheat in the wind,
   going from green to gold,
just the wheat & wind
   & me.

At 10 each morning
   the train would clang,
& once it left, no one,
   nothing moved,
nothing spoke—
birds or bugs
   or coyote.

Scary Ride
written with Manuel

I was young and biking in the snow.
   Night fell and I kept
having to stop. We were
   in the forest
in Washington State—
a railroad grade
   turned to a gravel path
& at the end a tunnel, like
   the end
or beginning
   of a life.

Baptism Sketch

After the water
  and the holy hand
on the forehead,
  Pastor Jeanie carries
the baby girl
  down the red aisle,
and Nora waves
  her little pink hand
like a princess
  in a parade.

Easy for Me

Sunday, and E is
   on his violin with those
high high notes
   that tremble
and sing, how kids
   know, feel
in those tremolo
   notes, notes
adults have trouble
   hitting, holding.

Trees Have Bark

E says, *Trees have bark—*
like a dog? How can
the two
  be true. E, at 4,
presses an ear
  to the trunk
of the tree.

Music

That Kind of Quiet

It's that kind of quiet
where you notice
the waves of a/c, the air
coming in and out of vents
in streams, that kind of quiet
where, if you listen, you can hear
your heartbeat, your lungs
filling. I like to wait
in this place, listen
for the buzzing of the world,
and not sleep, but wake.

Improv

The tie guy in the subway station
shows us the way, which train,
says, *From Kansas? What do you do?*
and I say, *Professor. Poet,* and he says,
Tell me one, and I'm quiet, shy, but do,
recite *Bird's Horn,* one of the only ones
I know by heart, smoothing the words
to him and the others in the subway car,
our hands clamped to the silver pole,
his head cocked my way, and he tells me
this is Parker's town, and I say,
We claim him, too, bop genius
born in KCK, cut his teeth in KCMO,
his fast jazz sound
stretching to the coast
like a cigarette ghost,
like a long flat cirrus cloud,
like an unending river
coming from the mouth
of his golden golden saxophone.
Coltrane said he didn't hear
double time till he heard Bird,
didn't know half
of the things you could do.

Jazz Standards

That sax, the bell of the horn, a little green, a trace
   of patina smoke—those tunes
don't rust, you can play
   till you're no longer blue
or even green.

Crazy

I know everyone,
every girl sings
Patsy's *Crazy*
at karaoke, but
in this little rusted-
out bar my drink
burns with your voice.

Knows Those Notes

Arms crossed, Brian
taps out the piano tune
on his arm in the pew,
his Sunday off.

How composed music hopes
to capture something
that happened once
by accident—
an improvisation
in the street
or in a 3 am club
or between two kids
shouting, clomping
after a ball.

When you carry in drums,
everyone looks at you.
You bring
the music,
the beat, an ancient
song, heart
thump, like bringing
an atomic clock
or bomb—
or turntable
and endless stack of LPs.

Quartet

One rooster struts,
and the other three
say, *Hey, take*
a stroll. We'll
follow,
we'll follow
where you go.

Cadenza

That piano solo
just a few notes
before the last
cymbal roll,
like a kiss
before you go,
so much more
than a cheek peck
or hand hold,
a send-off note
written on wind: *Come.*
Come again.

House Rule

That *Caprica*
　episode
where they gimp
　Papa's knees, that
door knock: 123,
Shostakovich
　also knew,
listened
　for that
SS knock
　with an ear,
　an eye,
　a life.

Disquiet

Mom Brings My Drum to Menninger's

How that
garage sale conga
held what I knew
and needed,
when I thumped
my story
across its skin.

And the orderlies
said, *That's ok, sonny.*
You can play that,
play that again.

Anti-D

There were many nights I did not sleep
but shut off the light, my wife's hand
on my head, my chest, and I'd meditate
through the darkness and into light
and stand and take the day
one step, another. I couldn't sleep,
and the pills came and brought me
darkness, and I'd no longer dream.

Take One, Take Two

My head's going crazy, so I take a pill
  from the big red bottle, a jagged one, two,
and J drives me through
  Wendy's, and I down those little pills
with Coke, take a gulp-
  ful, crinkle back the top, never
a straw, and I bite into that big burger,
hot meat and melted melted cheese,
ketchup, mustard on my chin, my cheek,
and eat it all in under a minute,
  and close my eyes, and thank my
wife, who puts a small hand
  on my thigh, drives.

Chipping, Backyard Golf

That summer, I tried to hit
trainer golf balls, the ones
with holes, over
my parent's house, chip-
ping from lawn
over driveway, avoiding
the house windows
and the gutter, if I
was lucky. Launch one
right over the house,
and I could sleep easy
at home again
in my kid bed,
my wife with
her people, parents.
Others, most, it felt
like diving
back into childhood,
spelunking, penniless,
penitent—together, but
so so alone.

Moving

When your things
are all in boxes, and you don't
want to go, when
tomorrow may not look
great as today, when
you're leaving and you get
handshakes and hugs, but no
kisses, you know
it has to be
time to move on.

Time Off

Meet me at the coffee shop, or victory lap

Having a black iced tea
by the window, the sky
a dappled grey; waiting
for my friend
in from Topeka, and we'll talk
& write & see a movie,
the semester done,
grades in, regalia
crumpled in the trunk.

Snowed in in NYC, Vacation Extended

We get snowed in,
 no flights out of NY
today or tomorrow, so we can't leave
until Wednesday, and will miss work,
and two poetry gigs,
but it could be worse,
to be stuck in NY
with family that live in Manhattan,
the snow coming down
like fat moths, angels
in mid-March, eight inches
that turns to slush in the sun
the next morning, the doormen
out with brooms and shovels,
and we trot the sidewalks,
the three of us, mittened, hand in hand,
happy. Family.

Off the Clock

And on that day, I clocked out
at 4, went with my friend
for coffee, for tea, let
the clock hands spin
for an hour
above my empty desk.

Alamo, KC

Do we need
  popcorn?

Can we ride
  the streetcar
all night?

Who was that
  you said
you loved?

On the Road

Rain coming, the black cows
lie down in the green and wait
for droplets, for a summer
shower like a lover's
touch, all hazy
and indigo, late June
in east central Kansas
along the turnpike, driving
the grey ribbon
that never ends.

Rush Hour Break

Went to
Subway, bought myself
10 or 15 minutes
to think
to write
to sit, watch
rush hour
cars line up
& drive by.

I got a six-inch
& water.
Cost me 5 dollars.

Seven Minute Break

From my office window
I can see out over
the trees, the tops of university
buildings, and to the highway
that leads to bigger towns.

The light is mild now
after a rain,
though it's hot, in the mid-90s,
and I can hear birdsong
beyond the a/c and fluorescent hum.

I don't know if I want
to be outside or sitting here,
but I know I've stopped all work
to look and wait
for signs.

Words, Language

Translation

When Murad calls, we turn Azerbaijani
into English, lines that have no translation
into something I might say—
if I were wilder, had darker dreams, had been
in prison and the poems came and went
with me, in the darkness behind a silhouette
of bars, and then in the light, the feet
of freedom. Murad calls, and I know somewhere
someone speaks in a tongue I will never know,
but my American friends can hear him,
when we set the words he's mouthed
on the page and turn them, like in a magic trick,
from paper into doves.

Word Bank

Years, I've held onto
   these words
for you. Here,
have a few.

Not Blocked

Sometimes, you must
be willing to just sit
there with your pen
above paper, and wait.

His Sentence

Teacher would tell
Don to cover the board
in sentences, his
sentence, then make him
erase every word. Don keeps
every one of his handwritten
notebooks now, hoards
words, erases
nothing.

Dialogue, Monologue

Always
at the coffee house
he talks, talks
and talks
to himself.

Underwater

When I went underwater
　in the tub
I heard voices, something up
　from the pipes.

On the Train to the Reading

On the train to Bellmore
   Beth rests her head
on Leo's shoulder, grins
when I take the shot,
   the camera crackled
into light. Leo
has unfurled his winter scarf,
   the lines on his forehead
loose, and we pass his childhood
   home on the rail, headed
to a coffee shop, where I'll read
   poetry from a music stand,
close as I may ever get
   to reading in NYC.

Dirty Kanza

Early enough, they put us
   under a tree, & we
write poems for bicyclists—
   80 in the shade: poems,
poems, poems for hire,
   words like a deep
sip of summer
   lemonade, syllables
like cicada call:
   come on, come on
     out of the sun.

Theatre Going

That white noise murmur
of the house with the lights up
before the show, what
heaven might be like
at first, before we know
the words.

I'd Like to Write

  thank you notes
all day—to (even) people
I've never met, thanking
each for the acts
  of their hands
& mouths, how
  they bring the good
of the world into being
  through action, at least
what I love so
so much about it.

Prose Sketches

Everyone Just Wants to Drum

On the sandwich board, it says *Clowns & Activities* with an arrow to the right. To the left, another arrow and *Poet Laureate*. I stand by my arrow, lucky tonight not to be too much of a clown, my books laid out on the table, my drums set up (I do a jazz poetry bit), my music stand raised and holding a speech and stack of poems. I'm in Mulvane, KS, down by Wichita, and there are about 300 people out for a library night, food trucks out back, face painting going on, and no one seems to be following the sign to me, and so I start in on my cajón, the low box drum, playing an inviting, but measured, Brazilian beat. Maybe someone will hear and be curious, and five minutes in a little kid comes with his mom, and I show them the drum, and the snare and cymbal set up in front, and they don't want to just talk; they want to play, and so I let the five year old slap his hands across the cajón's wooden top, then hand him a pair of cartwheel timpani mallets with socks over the tops as a muffler, and he plays the snare with the snares off, a tom tom, and gongs the cymbal, and we're off. I've lowered the snare stand for him, and he's standing tall, dancing even, as he plays, and hearing this, other kids come, hands tethered to their moms, then untethered, running, and there are kids on all of my drums, and I think I might need an Advil with the thrumming in my forehead, my temples, but it's ok, I know this sound, and it means the drums are beginning, given a start in their hearts, and about 50 kids make their way through in an hour, and, when it comes time to say and sing my poetry, only about six show up. Everyone just wants to drum.

Relic

Mondays, I visited Bird's Horn, that white plastic saxophone
he played once in Toronto, Parker who kept showing up
to gigs without a horn, and everyone would loan him one,
bop genius, fast-jazz man, hooked on junk after a car crash
coming from the Ozarks, and the doctor prescribed heroin
for the pain, which he never kicked. I volunteered days at
the American Jazz Museum, and there in the cave-like dark
behind lit glass, like a religious relic in angel-light, rested
Bird's Horn.

Write for an Hour at the Office

And, during the summer, what I had was time—an hour here or there, that if I ignored the looming, longer projects, I could bend to my own ends: work on a poem, start a short play, write a letter to a dear friend. Of course, I might be interrupted at any moment with a call from a prospective student, a call from my Dean, a stop-in, an urgent email, that sort of thing. But, right now, I'm using that hour, deciding to write, although I'm tired and would rather cruise the Net or read a book or watch part of a show on Kanopy. I'm deciding that I'd rather be a writer for an hour, if even an hour, than watch my life pass like a slow, cool car, everyone watching, but no one really noticing who's driving, what's going on inside: the passed out passenger in the back seat, the driver with his too-cool shades. A blur, a haze overtakes me in offices in the middle of the day in the summer. I'd rather be outside. I'd rather be listening to some good music, drinking some tea, watching the sun move slowly across the sky. I'd rather be reading something I love. I'd rather be watching the people come to the counter for their coffees and writing some of what I see and some of what is lodged in memory waiting to come out, given time and space, given voice by a kind of attitude: I'll sit here and listen to this.

About that time we left the locker room through a cloud

When Spindly held Sam up against the lockers, Spindly's fists at Sam's shoulders, pinning him, I thought of Spider-Man, how he would have cocked his legs and given Spindly a quick kick and sprung into the room, taken all of those pock-faced bullies out. Middle school was like that, bullies fighting their own faces—with razors and zit cream—then taking it all out on you, hoping to turn your face red, too. We learned to ball our fists when we heard our names. Don't wait. Don't get hit before you're ready to put at least one punch up, at least draw a purple bruise across a chin or chest, leave a mark before you go down. That way, you might not be the mark next time. That way, they know you have some scrap in you. We were all little. We were alone when gym was done, there in the locker room. The only time I saw gym-teach coach stop a fight, all he did was turn all of the shower heads on. The room soon a cloud, and the little ones, we fled first from the plume, as if behind us there'd been fire or a bomb. We never looked back, not for fear we'd turn to salt, but because everyone knows you run better if you never ever turn.

Song Cycle:
Poems at the Piano

Missing Moon

Moon gone, sun up, I wait
for your signal, a flash
of my mirror to your mirror,
using sunlight,
our signal, from window ledge
to window ledge—blackened,
quiet; we wait
for the glow of the moon—
no-moon night, deep-well-water night,
coal-colored night; our time
separate, with no lightning bug signals,
no mirror flashes between us.

Staccato Beans

She bought the beans,
and they jump, and they jump.
I cannot eat
beans that jump
past tongs of fork,
past edge of knife.

I use a spoon
as a mirror.

I watch them go.

Herd Boy's Song

My grandfather, Ollie,
went slow up the hill,
stick in hand, moving
with the cattle, his feet entrained
with their hooves. They step;
he steps. From water hole to hilltop,
from far field to the cattle path
that traces the skirt of the low hill,
my grandfather moved with the herd.

Blue Nun

Bertha went to see the Blue Nun
about Curtis, who she wanted
to drop off the roof. Blue Nun
said, *Don't do it. Even though
you're tempted like Abraham was
with Isaac. (Don't do it.) Use
a chicken instead.*

Ancient Burial

On top of the hill out back
the Indian scout is buried, his people
left scrapers and arrowheads
across the now-furrow-cut fields,
a mortar and pestle above
his head, top of hill, best spot
from which to see
the buffalo and the tribes
all on the move, traveling
below the high wind.

Floating Clouds

Above us, clouds
sag with rain, as if they
carry heavy sacks. They move now
with weight. Then, rain,
and those clouds run,
sleek and thin
on to another pasture, another
town, water
rising and following.

Red Wilderness

I am 13. It is an autumn
of prairie heather and milo
speckled red. A pheasant rooster
rises from the grasses and calls—
a battle cry squawk, beyond air,
beyond rain, almost beyond shot.
I shoot. He falls.

Sunrain

Grandma tells the legend:
the foxes marry when it rains,
when the sun is still up & bright.
Don't watch them
or you'll pay.
I walk the farm all day—
look for foxes.
No rain.

At the Gym, the Gas Station, the Coffee Shop

Curls

He pulls the bar
up from his waist
  to his face,
curls it, like
pulling a lover in
  for a hug or a kiss,
intimate
  with metal.

Grunt

They pull; they
  pump; they lift;
they grunt:
  *One more, one
more*, and swing
arms, try
  to fling
all of that pain out,
  and lift again
again again.

Power

for Lisa

Baby, Jane (Fonda) ain't got nothin'
   on you. You can
sweat with the best, use
   your beautiful body
(6, 7, 8) to teach
   us all how to move
(powerclean, upright row).
   When I watch you
it is like watching
   a toned goddess
splash from the sea,
   ocean-foam at your toes
instead of a plastic step
   and black foam mat.

Gas Station

The trucks
   queue up
at the pump
   Easter weekend,
everyone wanting
   to be anywhere
but here.

Gas Station Window Spot

When you sit
  by the door,
you know
  what's coming in—
summer gusts, winter wind.

Outside the Starbucks
   by the interstate,
trees that turned
   their limbs
from the wind grew away
   from the push
and movement
   of everyone going
everywhere
   so quickly, while they
stayed put, rooted
   moved
and immoveable.

How they
   watch us go.

How to Coffee Shop

That afternoon, he watched cars
out the coffee shop window
and didn't go anywhere
   until close,
drank slow
   and tipped big,
lived like everyday
   would be this way,
lived in endless endless sips.

Endless Iced Tea

If the baristas don't pay
too much attention to you,
use your water bottle
to top off your half-full
iced tea. Repeat, repeat.
See, you can drink
this way all day.

Our Songs

That afternoon, we sat outside
at Starbucks, drank iced tea
in the shade and wrote
our dreams, long
or short as they were, and let
the music above drift
into the street and into
the soccer fields and drive-thru queues
without listening. We were
making our own
music on paper
with pen and pencil.
That afternoon, the songs
were new, the songs
were ours.

Observations

Hum

Outside, the hum
  of mowers, evening
    coming on, family coming over
tomorrow, for some.

In the Well

When someone comes
with a flashlight,
what do you do—
call out or cover
your eyes?

That afternoon ...

... I ate my last burrito of the season.
... I let out a fart near some cheerleaders.
... I wrote through lunch.
... I bought tickets to a school musical.
... I almost got hit by a truck in the crosswalk.
... I rethought my life.

Commencement

We gathered 'round the fire
centuries ago—and danced.
　Now we sweat
in regalia robes, offer
a handshake, have you walk
the stage—to air horn blast,
to claps, to hoot and holler,
today—today—you're done.

Snow for Easter

Outside, again
  it grows cold, snow
for Easter, another way
  to hide eggs—
in drift & mound &
  hollowed out
hole.

Rain Day

During the grey day,
  rain day,
I forget everything, every-
  one, pull up
the covers till 11,
and wake to see the world
  underwater.

Hail

How the hail, pea-sized,
   froghops on the lawn,
bright white, rock-like, misshapen,
   and sounds like bags
of marbles being dropped
   on top the roof.

Now & Now & Now

The evening air
  unlike a/c
holds the memory
  of the sun …

clouds, days,
  but no rain, the sky
like concrete block …

I need to trim
  these front porch
bushes, so I can see
  to see.

Instances

It's not that
  there's never enough
to write about,
  but too much—
the red onion
  in silver moon slices
on top the spinach
  of my salad, something
to wake me
  from the lunch-hour haze;
the way the students
  take their backpacks
by one handle
  then ground or table
the pack, take
  a book, a paper
out; how River
  clops by in her new heels,
a zipped pouch
  of bills in one hand,
the week's earnings
  trotted to the bank;
how I can hear
  the oil sizzle,
French fries dipping in—
  and that tang
of salt and potato,
  how nothing
is quite like
  that instant scent.

More Than

What we read
are more
than notes, more than what
someone once said—
with a pen, with a bow,
a flute, a drum.

Branch, *The Learning Tree*

Newt holds
his stick, only thing
between him
and Marcus's fists,
almost how
the book
should end.

Reincarnate

Some people say
they'd rather
come back as a cat,
but I'd like
to be a magnolia branch
  in the wind
  in the summer,
green and pink and free,
  abloom.

NOTES:

DK Poems: "Hockey," "Golden Boy," "Wind in the Wheat," "Scary Ride," and "Dirty Kanza" were written at a poetry booth at the Dirty Kanza (DK) road race. I interviewed racers and observers, then turned their stories into poems. Some told stories about riding the gravel on off-road bicycles. Others talked about other things.

Song Cycle: Poems at the Piano: This batch of poems was written for pianist and professor Martin Cuellar as part of a collaboration. The first drafts were written on stage as part of a piano recital. Martin's student would play the piece, and I would write. The student would replay the piece, and I would read the poem aloud as part of the music. Each poem corresponds to a movement in a Tao Lin composition.

"Snowed in in NYC, Vacation Extended," "On the train to the reading," and "Improv" were written during our family trip to NYC in March 2018 to see Beth Moritz and Leonard Brauner. (Thanks, Beth and Leonard.)

"Translation" is for Murad Jalilov.

Kansas Poet Laureate (2017-2019), Kevin Rabas teaches at Emporia State University, where he leads the poetry and playwriting tracks and chairs the Department of English, Modern Languages, and Journalism. He has ten books, including *Lisa's Flying Electric Piano,* a Kansas Notable Book and Nelson Poetry Book Award winner, and *All That Jazz.*

www.ingramcontent.com/pod-product-compliance
Lightning Source LLC
Chambersburg PA
CBHW020124130526
44591CB00032B/515